SCOTTISH TRACTION

Colin J. Howat

AMBERLEY

First published 2017

Amberley Publishing
The Hill, Stroud
Gloucestershire, GL5 4EP

www.amberley-books.com

Copyright © Colin J. Howat, 2017

ISBN 978 1 4456 7374 5 (print)
ISBN 978 1 4456 7375 2 (ebook)

British Library Cataloguing in Publication Data.
A catalogue record for this book is available from
the British Library.

Origination by Amberley Publishing.
Printed in the UK.

Introduction

Following on from *Ayrshire Traction* and *Strathclyde Traction*, *Scottish Traction* covers the Scottish rail scene from 1974 until the present day. A lot has changed since the 1970s, with electrification slowly but surely expanding throughout the region.

This book covers diesel locos from humble Class 08s to Class 92s. On the DMU side I have covered classes 101 to 185s and EMUs covered are from Class 303 to 390s. On the electric loco side, classes 81 to 92 are covered. The AC electric loco fleets are not among the most popular to have operated over Scottish routes but like some of their contemporary diesel classes, they have played a major role in the modernisation of the rail system in Scotland.

The 100-strong first generation of AC electric locomotives were built to a common design theme stipulated by the British Transport Commission (BTC). Originally classified as AL1–AL5, the fleets were later classified 81–85 and were the backbone of the modernised electric routes until AL6 (Class 86) locomotives emerged in the mid-1960s. The first-generation electric fleets were not reliable and if it had not been for the extension of the WCML electrification to Glasgow Central in 1974, some would certainly have been withdrawn much earlier than they were. Fortunately, a member of each of the pioneering classes has been saved from the breaker's yard and are currently under the custodianship of the AC Electric Loco Group based at Barrow Hill, Staveley, Chesterfield. Of these, the preserved Class 84 is also part of the National Rail collection.

As part of the 1955 BTC Modernisation Plan, it was announced by the Labour Government that all future electrification projects would be standardised on the industrial frequency AC system. This included the Glasgow suburban lines on both the north and south side of the Clyde. In terms of locomotives, a new mixed-traffic standardised design was to be established. It was also necessary that sections of the catenary wire were energised at different voltages where certain bridges had limited clearances, necessitating lower voltages. The pantographs, however, could run under a continuous wire system, including neutral sections.

The mechanical design of the AC loco fleet came from various directives by the BTC with major input from industrial design companies. Some major limitations were imposed, leading to severe restraints on manufacturers' design freedom. The restrictive UK loading gauge was the main one but other stipulations included a need for 48-inch diameter wheels, a flat lower roof to house pantographs, and a 20 ton maximum axle load. This produced a range of locos with a strong family likeness. All had standard driving cabs, most used the same auxiliary equipment and as result performance of each class was very similar. At an early stage in the design process, weight calculations showed that axle loadings could be exceeded and this led to a considerable redesign and changes to equipment, which delayed deliveries of all locos. All the early AC locos had bogie-frame-mounted traction motors, which required flexible drives to keep the un-sprung weight on the axles to a minimum.

Although the orders for the first 100 locomotives were placed in the mid-1950s, design and construction was very slow, with the first locos not being delivered until 1959. Hyndland Depot on the north side of Glasgow took over the maintenance of Class 303s, or the Blue Trains as they became known. Later on, Shields Depot on the south side of Glasgow opened in 1967, also for Class 303s and new Class 311s, which had been introduced on the Gourock and Wemyss Bay to Glasgow Central lines. Later on, from January 1975, this depot also maintained the Class 81s.

The Class 81s suffered from body lean caused by faults in the body support springs. This caused excessive lateral movement, causing the loco body to make contact with the rubber bogie lateral stops. Various modifications were carried out to reduce this problem. However, a high number of complaints were received from drivers about bad riding and this resulted in a test run between Glasgow Shields Depot and Beattock in the winter of 1977. This resulted in a further batch of modifications to reduce lateral movement and bounce. The Class 81s remained in service on the WCML until 1991, when the remaining handful were withdrawn.

The single largest class of electric locomotive ever ordered in the UK was the AL6, later known as Class 86. Ordered in the mid-1960s, this class followed the same design principle as the earlier Class 81–85s. After initial riding problems at high speed, a massive rebuilding programme was instigated in the early 1970s, which culminated in revised bogie springing. They were the mainstay of the WCML until they were replaced by the later Class 87 and 90 locos. The Class 86s also suffered from the use of axle-hung traction motors with high un-sprung weights at high-speed operation. This was found to be damaging track, resulting in a spate of broken rails, which were attributed to the impact of the locos. An interesting development was the fitting of multiple control and TDM push-pull equipment. In the late 1980s and early 1990s, a number of Class 86/4s were dedicated to freight traffic. As a result, these locos had their train heating isolated and vacuum brakes removed and their top speed was reduced to 75 mph.

The Class 86/6 sub-class was introduced from 1989 for freight-only operation. When originally built, the early examples were finished in electric blue – the first handful without yellow warning panels, which were soon added. The first new livery to appear was in 1984 with the unveiling of the InterCity business sector colours, which were grey and white with red body stripes. This was subsequently followed by several variations, culminating in the standard InterCity Swallow livery in 1989. The Railfreight sector introduced a new two-tone grey livery in 1986 followed by a revised Railfreight distribution colour from 1992. This was also replaced by Rail Express Systems (RES) livery from 1993. Following privatisation in 1996, locos operated by Virgin West Coast services and CrossCountry were quickly repainted in the red/grey house colours of Virgin. Those allocated to the Anglia route were repainted in turquoise while members of the Freightliner were painted green. A handful of locos emerged in EWS red and gold. The operating area for Class 86s had been quite restricted mainly due to the limits of electrification. However, as the electrified network spread and expanded in 1973 from Carlisle to Glasgow Central, 86s started to penetrate further north. With the electrification of the East Coast Main Line (ECML) between 1985 and 1990, the class made various appearances, visiting Edinburgh on the newly electrified route from Carstairs. On the West Coast Main Line (WCML), 86s remained in charge of main line services from the days of British Rail right through to privatisation and operation by Virgin Trains.

The Class 87 electric locos, or Electric Scots as they were originally termed, were ordered and built by British Rail in partnership with GEC traction at BREL Crewe. This fleet, along with classes 81 to 86, became the prime power for the WCML from May 1974. Soon after introduction BR relaxed the ban on naming locos and all these locos received nameplates very quickly. They remained at the forefront with Class 90s until Virgin Trains replaced them with Class 390 Pendilenos. The Class 90s were originally ordered as a replacement for the Class 87s for use on both passenger and freight work. Their superior traction characteristics saw the fleet an immediate success. The remainder of this fleet was divided between EWS and Freightliner. Some are still used today on the Caledonian Sleepers and freight work and continue to play a vital part in the UK railway scene.

The Class 92s were specifically built for use through the Channel Tunnel, both on passenger and freight, and later services to and from Scotland. By July 1996 UK safety approval had been granted for Class 92s to enter revenue-earning service. However, the first use of a Class 92 on a passenger service did not come until 12 July 1997, when No. 92030 operated a Hertfordshire Railtours Special from London to Kent. After DB Schenker, most of the Class 92 fleet are now operated by DB Cargo. A number have also been exported to Eastern Europe where there is a large demand for powerful electric locos. Some of the fleet are also owned by GB Railfreight and have been used on the Caledonian Sleeper services.

Class 08s were the most common shunting locomotives in Scotland but are fast becoming a rarity on our current rail system, with the larger main-line locos performing the job of marshalling trains. The basic design came from the pre-war locomotives operated by most of the Big Four railway companies. The BR standard diesel-shunting loco was a direct follow on of the final LMS design. Using 350 hp, these shunters went on to prove to be a very reliable, strong and simple loco to operate. Over 1,000 locos were built and examples could be found in all corners of Scotland.

By far the most successful of the early diesels was the English Electric Class 20. They were ordered under the Modernisation Plan of the 1950s and were known as the Type 1s. They had a single cab and later became reclassified as Class 20. These locos were built at both the Vulcan Foundry at Newton-le-Willows and at the Robert Stephenson & Hawthorns Ltd factory at Darlington. Some of the fleet became very reliable and were well-liked by train crews, with their versatility allowing them to operate in pairs or on their own. Their performance saw them outlast all other small Type 1 locos and they can still be found on the UK network. A small batch of Class 20s were taken over in 1988 by Hunslet Barclay, based in Kilmarnock, for weed-control train operation, and were some of the first private locos to be authorised over BR tracks. Under privatisation the fleet saw a new lease of life, with over twenty bought by Direct Rail Services, based at Carlisle. Many others were taken over by various private operators. A small number also saw use in the building of the Channel Tunnel.

Type 2 locos, later classified Class 24 and 25, were designed by BR as a replacement for lower-powered steam traction. The Standard Type 2 fleet eventually ran to 478 locomotives. They were built over a 10-year period, starting in 1958. To speed up production, Class 24 and 25 locomotives were constructed at BR Derby, Crewe and Darlington. A small batch were also constructed by Beyer Peacock. The standard Type 2s were a true universal design and operated throughout the UK, from the Southern Region in Kent to the north of Scotland. Some of the Class 25 locos were converted to electric train heating locos (ETHEL) in the mid-1980s for use on the West Highland Line when there was a shortage of ETS-fitted Class 37s.

As another result of the 1950s modernisation plan, Class 26 and 27 locos were built by the Birmingham Carriage and Wagon Works. These locos were originally delivered to the Eastern Region, where they took over suburban and outer suburban services. Other Class 26 and 27s were delivered new to Scotland while other batches were delivered to the London Midland Region. After a few months in service, the British Rail Board (BRB) decided to transfer all these locos to depots in Scotland. With the modernisation of the important Edinburgh to Glasgow Queen Street line taking place, high-speed running of this route was undertaken in the late 1960s with Class 27s and later Class 37s. The BRB eventually agreed to deploy pairs of modified Class 27s operating top and tail with rakes of modified Mk 2 coaching stock to replace the ageing Class 126 DMUs. The locos were fitted with electric train supply (ETS). Sadly the hammering received on this route led to some unreliable performances, but in time they settled down and worked well until they were replaced in October 1979 by the more powerful Class 47s and Mk 3 coaching stock. Both the Class 26 and 27s remained in front-line service in Scotland until 1993 and 1987 respectively. Thankfully, a sizeable number have been preserved.

The Class 33s were built by the Birmingham Carriage & Wagon Company and were one of the most popular diesel locos of all time. They were based in England and I mention them simply because in the twilight of their careers some ventured into Scotland on various specials. The same applies to the Class 58 locos. Again based in England, a few ventured into Scotland on coal workings on the ECML and on the odd special.

The popular English Electric Class 37s were introduced from 1960 and went on to number 309 in total. Nobody would have thought back then that they would still be in service over fifty years later. Under the initial orders placed by the BRB, no provision was made for locomotives within the 1,500 to 1,800 hp range. It quickly emerged that a more powerful locomotive above the Type 2s was required. Orders were placed with English Electric for Type 3 power, which later became the Class 37. In common with the majority of standard UK locomotives, the design incorporated a driving cab position at each end in the then English Electric practice. A nose or bonnet section was also provided ahead of the cab areas to accommodate air compressors, traction motor blowers, and vacuum exhausters. Later locos also had horns roof-mounted centrally between the middle cab windows. When introduced, the maximum service speed was 90 mph, although some specified locomotives were temporarily authorised at higher speeds as part of acceleration trials.

From the early 1960s, some were sent to Scotland for the first time. Members of the class were allocated to Polmadie, Eastfield and Haymarket depots. Some that had been transferred were considered for push-pull working between Glasgow Queen Street and Edinburgh. During the 1970s, the Class 37s settled down to become the backbone power of the UK rail network. Major refurbishments and life extensions continued in the 1980s and many can still be found on passenger and freight work. They will probably be best remembered in Scotland growling up and down between Ravenscraig Steelworks and Hunterston iron ore and coal workings from 1978 until 1992.

Class 44–46 diesels, or Peaks, were introduced again in the early 1960s. Ten locos (Class 44) were allocated to Derby but were soon transferred to Camden in London. When the production locos, later Class 45s, emerged from Derby and Crewe Works, the majority were allocated to Derby, Cricklewood in London and Toton. The Class 46s were similar to their sister Class 45s, but with a few modifications. The Peak family remained largely on the Midland Main Line until they were displaced by the new HSTs from 1982. Most of them visited Scotland via the Waverley and G&SW routes. However, they were eventually banned from Glasgow Central from 1981 after a number of derailments in the jungle area outside the station.

Class 50s were introduced from 1968. They were the first main-line diesels to be delivered in all-Rail Blue. After completion of the WCML to Glasgow Central in 1974, they were transferred to the Western Region. Most of the Class 50s ventured all over the south-west of Scotland and were to be seen regularly between Dumfries and Kilmarnock and even as far south as Girvan and as far north as Inverness. These locos had slow speed control fitted but as the class were rarely employed on freight work this was hardly ever used. They were fitted for multiple operation and a total of fifty were made. After being transferred to the Western Region from 1974, most never ventured back to Scotland, apart from a few that returned on specials. Most ended up at the breaker's yard at MC Processors at Springburn in Glasgow.

Possibly the ultimate in the early diesels was the Class 55 or the Deltics. They were introduced from May 1961 on the East Coast Main Line (ECML) and also worked north of Edinburgh to and from Aberdeen. Occasional flurries resulted in visits to the Central Scotland area. From 1978 HSTs began to take over from them on expresses from Edinburgh to London Kings Cross and the Deltics began to spread to other parts of the country. On several occasions during the summer of 1979 they were even diverted over the Glasgow & South Western Line via Dumfries and Kilmarnock due to various problems on both the ECML and WCML. Throughout their careers, the 55s had very few modifications apart from the fitting of electric train heating (ETS). In 1968 the BRB decided that the future of high-speed rail in the UK lay in unit formations, so even the Deltics' lives had already been mapped out.

The Class 56 locos were introduced from 1976 as there was a need for a dedicated freight locomotive due to various external factors, including high fuel prices exacerbated by the then Middle East crisis. The BRB were instructed by the government to get more coal transported between the mines and the power stations and this resulted in the birth of the Class 56 loco. The original sixty locomotives were provided by Electroputere of Craiova in Romania. The rest of the fleet was built by BREL at Crewe. Many of these locos survived well into the privatisation era, but by April 2004 the last official workings in the UK took place. Since then a number of the locos have been taken on by Colas and various other private operators and some have been exported.

Following sectorisation of BR in the late 1980s, it was soon identified that a heavy freight locomotive was needed. An order was placed with Brush Traction of Loughborough for 100 Class 60 locos. Sadly, after privatisation and the takeover of the UK rail freight business by American-owned Wisconsin Central, the Class 60 design fell out of favour and many of them were destined to be stored indefinitely at Toton depot, near Nottingham. Later, under DB control, consideration was given to scrap the entire Class 60 fleet. However, a turn of fortune spearheaded by UK engineers saw the Super 60 project and since 2013 over twenty locos have been returned to traffic. Most of this class have been seen in Scotland, particularly on the busy Ayrshire coal workings.

The success of the Class 59 in the mid-1990s on aggregate trains made EWS decide around 1995 to start importing Class 66s, which were built in Ontario, Canada. Deliveries of the Class 66 started in early 1998, with batches usually of twelve being delivered via the port of Immingham. The new locos were built with standard pneumatic buffers, a central coupling hook and shackle, one main reservoir and one air brake pipe mounted on the draw beam. From loco No. 66201, swing-head semi-auto couplers were installed from new, with all pre-delivered locos also fitted. Deployment in the UK was rapid, with the entire EWS network quickly seeing Class 66 activity. The first Freightliner locos, No. 66501 and No. 66502, were delivered to the UK in July 1999. Due to winning an infrastructure contract from Railtrack, Freightliner ordered a further eighteen Class 66 locos. From 2002 other operators such as GBRF and DRS also ordered these locos and by the end of 2003 Freightliner had continued to add more to its fleet, reaching a total of fifty locos. By the summer of 2004, GBRF placed another order and the success story continued with further deliveries being made.

The Class 67 fleet emerged as a direct result of the UK rail privatisation process and they were ordered by EWS. It was quickly agreed that a new motive power was required to operate in the UK freight sector, mainly on high-speed trains. EWS again turned to General Motors. They stipulated that they needed a loco capable of 125 mph with electric train heating based on a four-axle bogie. General Motors were agreeable and a partnership was formed with Alstom. EWS ordered thirty Class 67s, which were assembled at the Alstom plant in Valencia, Spain. All were delivered by the year 2000. The locos were immediately deployed on Royal Mail contract services but sadly in 2004 this work was lost. From 2004 the Class 67s took over the diesel legs of the ScotRail Sleeper services to Inverness and Aberdeen and from 2006 the Fort William portions. Further passenger work came from ScotRail on Fife Circle services due to shortages of DMUs.

High Speed Trains (HST) or Class 43 locos were designed as a short-term answer for the need for the new long-distance modern trains required to compete with the growing motorway network and short-haul air travel. In the early 1970s the prototype High Speed Diesel Train was designed and built at Crewe and Derby as a dynamic design and refinement tool before production trains were sanctioned. The introduction of the prototype train was delayed following major trade union issues relating to manning at high speeds, with ASLEF demanding two drivers on trains travelling at over 100 mph. The BRB's wish for 161 seven- or eight-car HST sets was rejected by the government of the time and eventually just ninety-five sets were built. However, with time these sets demonstrated that they were well suited to the internal UK high-speed market and went on to be the backbone of the InterCity network.

The anti-rail Conservative Government in the early 1980s halted many plans to develop a UK version of the Japanese High Speed Rail network, which would have linked the most important and heavily populated locations around the UK. This was rejected even though the cost per mile at the time of a twin-track railway was less than that of equivalent motorway construction. It was soon realised by the BRB that with no government support for an improved railway in the UK, effort had to be made to try and raise speeds on the existing rail network without compromising safety. Major track works took place at a number of key locations with the ironing out of restrictive curves, which allowed slight train speed increases, while in other situations canting of the track was adopted, which also increased speeds as well. Mk 2 coaching stock then emerging from the BREL Derby Works were upgraded to operate at 100 mph; this included improvements to the bogies and suspension, which led the way to the Mk 3 coaching stock that would later be used with the HST sets. In May 1970 the BRB gave £70,000 to the development of the HST project. The BRB stated at the time that this would be a stop-gap measure until new electric, advanced passenger trains were ready, which was expected from the early 1980s. With no single diesel available to give the required 4,500 hp, it was agreed that two power cars, one at each end of a formation with a reduced 2,250 hp, would be the way forward. Developments of through train control made it possible for both engines to be used for traction and auxiliary power at the same time. Paxman, based at Colchester, were able to offer a suitable twelve-cylinder Paxman Valenta engine. The design of the brake system was a fundamental part of the HST concept. Design specification called for a train travelling at 125 mph to be able to stop the same distance as a conventional train travelling at a 100 mph.

The driving cabs were made of glass fibre reinforced with plastic constructed to 50 mm thickness, affording train crews the best possible protection at maximum speeds. The large single front windscreen was a laminated high-impact-resistant glass capable of withstanding a 2 lb block of steel impacting on the screen at up to 186 mph. From the outset, HSTs were to use a totally new design of coaches. The body structure was formed of a steel frame with a welded stressed steel skin. The design was carried out at Derby. To maintain the air-smooth and streamlined aesthetic appearance of the train, all underside equipment between the bogies were mounted in easy-to-remove modules with either hinged or detachable exterior doors.

By early 1973 all the prototype HST vehicles had been delivered from Derby Litchurch Lane. Later in the year, on 2 August, a special was run from London Kings Cross to Darlington, which included Richard Marsh, Chairman of the then BRB. Various MPs and press from all over the world also travelled on the special. The train was put through its paces and hit 125 mph south of York. The prototype was then split into different parts for further research, with the power cars being kept for further testing and development work. This included main-line running in connection with the Advanced Passenger Train (APT) on the West Coast Main Line. Other work included test runs with Mk 3 stock on the Western Region. By the summer of 1985, power car prototype 43000 was handed over to the National Railway Museum in York, where it was cosmetically restored to full working order.

A further twenty-seven HST sets were introduced to the Eastern Region from the beginning of 1978, with certain sets allocated to Edinburgh Craigentinny. The first set arrived at Heaton Depot, Newcastle, in August 1977. It had been planned to upgrade the power on these units but technical issues, compounded by the desire to maintain a common fleet, saw the upgrade cancelled.

The success of the HST fleet continued and by the late 1970s the BRB submitted further requests to the government for more sets due to severe overcrowding, particularly on the Eastern Region. Authority was granted but the order was reduced by the government. By 1980 there was a decrease in passengers travelling due to various reasons which allowed easier diagramming of sets, particularly on the Western Region. HSTs were finally transferred to the Midland Main Line from the end of 1982 and in the same years HSTs were diagrammed to/from Inverness and Aberdeen. Other sets have been diagrammed in Scotland between Glasgow Queen Street and London Kings Cross via Edinburgh and others have plied their trade over the WCML for CrossCountry. Others have even worked over the G&SW between Kilmarnock and Dumfries on booked and diverted CrossCountry services. Following the electrification of the ECML in 1989, most HST sets were re-shuffled around the country but many still operate in Scotland today, mostly being used between Inverness and Aberdeen to London Kings Cross. Most were replaced by Class 221/222 Voyagers from 2005. However, the Class 43s are arguably the most successful diesel locomotive ever made in the UK.

The first generation DMU fleets have never generated the huge following and interest as main line diesel and electric locomotives. However, today, with a reducing number of locomotives to follow, the older DMU stock has attracted more enthusiasts and this has been reflected in the large numbers of vehicles that are now preserved and in operation on a vast number of preserved railways. Again as part of the post-war plans, the British Transport Commission (BTC) stated that a cheaper diesel type of multiple unit was required to replace the ageing steam fleet on rural and branch lines. However, such was the haste in which the BTC required new trains in service that the BR workshops at Derby and Swindon could not cope with demand. As a result, the private sector workshops of Cravens, Gloucester RCW, Metro Cammell, Park Royal, Birmingham RCW, Wickams and Pressed Steel were all awarded contracts to build sets as well.

Not all of the new multiple unit trains were successful; some units had novel features that rendered them nonstandard and others suffered from poor production quality. With diesel units coming from a wide variety of suppliers, little standardisation emerged and thus the cost of maintaining the fleets also grew. By the time the full fleets were delivered, the UK railways had changed and many branch lines in Scotland had closed, while other routes had been altered, which meant a very short life for some of them. However, some very good high-quality trains emerged and these saved many lines and services from early closure.

DEPOT CODES

AK – Ardwick Manchester
AY – Ayr
BN – Bounds Green London
BR – Bristol Bath Road
CD – Crewe Diesel
CE – Crewe Electric
CK – Corkerhill Glasgow
CL – Colas Rugby
CZ – Central Rivers Burton
DE – Dundee
DT – Dunfermline Townhill
DR – DRS Carlisle
DY – Etches Park Derby
ED – Eastfield Glasgow
FL – Freightliner Leeds
GB – GB Railfreight Doncaster
GD – Gateshead
GW – Shields Depot Glasgow
HA – Haymarket
HM – Healey Mills
HN – Hamilton Depot
HQ – Headquarters (BR)
HT – Heaton
HY – Hyndland Glasgow
IM – Immingham
IS – Inverness
KD – Carlisle Kingmoor (BR)
LA – Plymouth Laira
LO – Longsight Manchester
NH – Newton Heath Manchester
NL – Neville Hill Leeds
PO – Privately Owned
SF – Stratford London
SP – Springs Branch Wigan
TE – Thornaby Tees
TI – Tinsley Sheffield
TO – Toton Nottingham
WC – West Coast Railways
WN – Willesden London
YK – York

A Class 86 at Glasgow Central awaits departure with the 19.30 postal service to London Euston. This was the train that the Great Train Robbers stole approximately £2.6 million in cash from on 8 August 1963. Taken July 1979.

No. 40047 (YK) passes over the Montrose Bridge with the 09.35 Glasgow Queen Street to Aberdeen service. This loco was withdrawn from traffic in November 1984. Taken October 1979.

Six-car 126 approaches Barassie station with an Ayr to Glasgow Central service. The signal box was closed in November 1982. Taken June 1979.

Three-car 116 at Ardrossan Winton Pier station with an afternoon service to Glasgow Central. A new platform was built approximately 200 metres away, on the Kilwinning side of the old Winton Pier location. This new station was opened upon commencement of the new Ayrshire electric services from January 1987. Taken July 1979.

No. 303051 (HY) arrives at Bellgrove with a Springburn to Milngavie service. This unit was withdrawn from traffic in 1987 after being involved in a crash with loco No. 37011 at Singer. Taken July 1979.

Three-car 107 departs from Shotts station with an Edinburgh to Glasgow Central service. At the time of writing this line is being electrified and will see electric traction from 2019, probably using Class 385s. Taken July 1979.

No. 311106 (GW) departs from the old Platform 13 at Glasgow Central with a service to Wemyss Bay. This platform was renumbered to 15 in October 2010. Taken October 1979.

Three-car 126 at Annan with the 14.10 Carlisle to Ayr service. This service ran from May 1979 until May 1983. Class 101 and 107 units took over from May 1982. Taken December 1979.

Six-car 107, unit No. 133 (HM) leading, crosses the River Irvine with an Ayr to Glasgow Central service. Taken June 1980.

No. 303045 (HY) at Glasgow Queen Street Low Level with an Airdrie to Balloch Central service. Taken June 1980.

Gloucester single-rail car No. 55000 (DE) approaches Arbroath with a service from Dundee. This single diesel unit escaped the scrapyard and is preserved at the South Devon Railway. Taken August 1980.

No. 46006 (LA) at Irvine Yard with a cement train to Eastgate, County Durham. This train was worked by Edinburgh Millerhill drivers. This area is long gone and the factory in the background was demolished to make way for a Tesco superstore. Beyond the rear of the train the line continued to Kilmarnock but this was lifted in 1969. Taken December 1979.

No. 311101 (GW) departs Glasgow Central with a service to Lanark. These services were re-directed to run via the Argyle line from November 1979 but reverted back to Glasgow Central High Level from May 2015. Taken August 1979.

Six-car 126 at Bogside, north of Irvine, with a Glasgow Central to Ayr service. Note the headcode still in use at this time (1A37). Bogside station closed in January 1967. Taken October 1975.

Three-car 126 at Irvine station with a Glasgow Central to Ayr service. Taken October 1980.

Three-car 107 departs from Fairlie High with a Largs to Glasgow Central service. The sidings on the left were used for nuclear flask traffic until the late 1990s. This line was singled when the line was electrified in January 1987. Taken November 1980.

Three-car 116 east of Kilmacolm with the 11.07 Glasgow Central via Paisley Canal service. This service was withdrawn in January 1983. Taken November 1980.

Three-car 116 passes Paisley Canal signal box with a Kilmacolm to Glasgow Central service. Taken November 1980.

107 power car No. 52011 (HM) undergoing refurbishment at Glasgow Works. Taken June 1981.

Six-car 107 at Giffen station with a Branch Line Society Railtour, which visited many branch lines around south-west Scotland. This line is now severed from the main line network at Lugton. Taken August 1981.

No. 105375 (HA) at Cardenden with a service to Edinburgh. Taken August 1981.

No. 47637 (IS) approaches Kilwinning Junction with the 17.12 Glasgow Central to Ayr service. Note the Mk 1 Sealink coaches painted to publicise the boat connections to and from Stranraer Harbour. This was a fill-in turn for the coaches between boat duties. The coaches were dual-braked and dual-heated but were eventually replaced in 1987 by Mk 2 coaches. Taken May 1984.

The Advanced Passenger Train (APT) at Glasgow Central with the 07.00 service to London Euston. The train was timed to take four hours to London – a time still unbeatable at the time of writing. These trains had many teething problems and were eventually withdrawn from traffic in 1985. Taken November 1982.

No. 47708 (HA) near Perth Yard with a special shuttle train from Perth station to Perth Yard in connection with a BR open day. Taken May 1985.

HST unit, with power car No. 43158 (NL) leading, arrives at Aberdeen with the 07.20 service from Leeds. Taken March 1990.

No. 26022 (IS) with a BG and local cleaner at Wick station. Taken August 1981.

No. 40162 (KD) at Irvine Yard shunting PCA cement wagons. The wagons were loaded at Irvine and this train would travel to Eastgate via Paisley, Shotts and Millerhill and then down the ECML. Taken June 1982.

No. 31215 (TE) arrives at Falkland Yard with a Speedlink Freight service from Carlisle Kingmoor Yard. This traffic ceased around 1991. Taken March 1987.

No. 55008 (YK) pulls away from Dundee with the 16.10 Aberdeen to York service. The train is approximately half a mile from the Tay Bridge. No. 55008 was withdrawn from traffic in December 1981 and was broken up at Doncaster Works by June 1982. Taken August 1981.

No. 86258 (WN) *Talwyn* with a dead Class 87 inside arrives at the Suburban platform at Edinburgh with the sleeper from London Euston. Taken February 1996.

No. 60046 (TO) at Drem with a steel coil train from Scunthorpe to Millerhill Yard. This loco is still in service with DB Cargo but its future is uncertain. Taken June 2004.

GNER HST at Larbert North with the 07.50 Inverness to London Kings Cross service. Taken September 2007.

No. 08761 (DE) at Dundee on station pilot duties. Note the Class 101 DMU in the background. Taken August 1981.

No. 81013 (GW) at Springburn Works. This loco was at the works in connection with another BR open day. The loco started life as No. E3015 and was renumbered to No. 81013 in August 1973. It was withdrawn from traffic in August 1989 after sustaining fire damage at Birmingham New Street. It was another loco sent for disposal at Tinsley Yard and was cut up by December 1991. Taken June 1981.

No. 85034 (CE) approaches Gretna Junction with a parcels train from Mossend Yard to Manchester Red Bank. This loco was withdrawn from traffic in October 1990. It was sent to Spingburn Works and cut up by January 1993. Taken May 1983.

GNER HST at Edinburgh Park station with the morning Inverness to London Kings Cross service. Taken November 2013.

A double-headed 86 and 87 combination crosses the border at Gretna Junction with a Mossend to Dee Marsh steel coil train. The steel originated from Ravenscraig steelworks, which was closed in 1992. Taken May 1983.

No. 86432 (WN) near Crawford with a Glasgow/Edinburgh to Manchester/Liverpool southbound express. This loco was named *Brookside* at Liverpool Lime Street in August 1987. It was renumbered No. 86632 in August 1989 and is still in service with Freightliner. Taken September 1985.

No. 66303 and No. 66422 (both DR) at Ballochmyle, south of Mauchline, with the Tesco train, the 06.15 Daventry to Grangemouth Intermodal service. This service was a diversion off the WCML due to Storm Frank. Taken February 2016.

No. 47550 (IS) *University of Dundee* at Montrose with the 10.55 Aberdeen to Glasgow Queen Street service. Taken December 1982.

No. 47709 (HA) *The Lord Provost* crosses the Forth Bridge with a southbound passenger service. Taken April 1987.

No. 47704 (HA) *Dunedin* at Gleneagles with the 13.40 Edinburgh to Perth service. This loco was sold to Waterman Railways in May 1994. It was eventually cut up by Ron Hull of Rotherham by December 2006. Taken October 1983.

No. 27045 (ED) emerges from Drumlanrig Tunnel between Sanquhar and Thornhill with the 13.45 Glasgow Central to Carlisle service. Taken October 1984.

No. 37028 (ED) passes Holywood signal box north of Dumfries with a northbound parcels service from London Euston to Stranraer Harbour. Parcels traffic ceased in the late 1980s. Taken October 1984.

No. 33109 and No. 33116 (Both SF) at Motherwell station with a railtour from Inverness to London Euston, organised by Hertfordshire Railtours. Taken Spring 1995.

No. 47309 (TI) bypasses the old Penmanshiel Tunnel with an Edinburgh to Newcastle local service. The original tunnel collapsed in March 1979, requiring both road and rail routes to be realigned. Taken July 1981.

No. 56004 (TO) at Falkland Yard with a loaded MGR from Killoch Colliery to Drax Power Station working. This was the last Class 56 to retain Rail Blue. It was cut up at Booths of Rotherham in July 2006. Taken September 1998.

No. 47565 (CD) *Responsive* at Glasgow Central Platform 11, having just arrived with a postal ECS train from Polmadie Depot to form the 19.30 service to London Euston. Taken July 1997.

No. 20148 and No. 20114 (Both ED) arrive at Aviemore with a southbound mixed Speedlink from Inverness Yard to Mossend Yard. Taken August 1984.

No. 37025 (ED) at Inverness with the 12.30 Inverness to Glasgow Queen Street service. No. 37025 was named *Quality Assured* at Bescot depot in May 1995. This loco is still in service with Colas. Taken August 1984.

No. 90004 (WN) *City Of Glasgow* arrives at Glasgow Central with ECS from Polmadie Depot to form a London Euston service. The loco was named at the station in August 1999. It was transferred to Anglia Railways in 2004 and still works for this company. Taken May 2003.

No. 55022/D9000 (PO) with No. 27052 (HA) and No. 20078 (ML) approach Perth station. These locos were all on display for the BR open day at Perth Yard. Taken April 1985.

No. 47424 (ED) approaches Inverness among an array of semaphore signals with the 10.20 service from Glasgow Queen Street via Aberdeen. Taken August 1981.

No. 47528 (YK) at Cockburnspath, just north of the border, on the East Coast Main Line with the 09.10 Dundee to London Kings Cross service. Taken July 1981.

HST at Burnmouth on the East Coast Main Line south of Dunbar, with No. 43098 (NL) leading, working an Edinburgh to London Kings Cross service. Taken July 1981.

A Class 86 arrives at Motherwell with the 15.02 Glasgow Central to Liverpool Lime Street service. Taken March 1981.

No. 92009 (CE) *Elgar* passes Carstairs with a Daventry to Coatbridge Freightliner service. This loco is still in use with DB Cargo. Taken March 2004.

No. 90017 (CE) arrives at Edinburgh with a service from North Berwick. Taken August 2005.

No. 20104 and No. 20105 (both HA) approach Mossend Yard with a coal train from Polkemmet Colliery, near Shotts. Taken May 1982.

No. 305501 (GW) arrives at Haymarket with a service from North Berwick. Taken June 2001.

Left: No. 40197 (HA) at Elderslie, south of Paisley, with a Grangemouth to Riccarton loaded oil tank train. This train had just come off the Paisley Canal Branch. Taken November 1980.

Below: No. 92019 (CE) at Lamington with a Daventry to Grangemouth Tesco train. This loco was named *Wagner* without ceremony at the Brush Traction Facility. It is still in service with DB Cargo. Taken August 2014.

No. 20039 and No. 27110 (both ED) near Barony Junction, north of Auchinleck, with a loaded MGR service from Barony Colliery to Longannet Power Station. Normally at this time, two Class 20s worked all the MGR traffic. Presumably the Class 27 was stepped up because of a Class 20 failure, which led to this unusual combination. Barony Colliery closed in 1983 and the signal box controlling movements to and from the colliery was finally removed by June 1986. Taken October 1980.

No. 60011 (TO) is near Mossblown, between Annbank Junction and Ayr, with a loaded MGR working from Killoch Colliery to Ayr Harbour. Taken August 1997.

No. 47431 (CD) at Inverkeithing with the 12.40 Aberdeen to Edinburgh service. Taken August 1981.

No. 91019 (BN) at Kirkhill with a diverted London Kings Cross to Glasgow Central service. This service was diverted due to engineering work in the Newton area. Taken January 1995.

No. 87017 (WN) *Iron Duke* passes Newton station with the 07.45 London Euston to Glasgow Central service. Taken May 1982.

No. 87021 (WN) *Robert The Bruce* passes over the Clyde, near Crawford, with a northbound London Euston to Glasgow Central service. Taken July 1981.

No. 318257 (GW) stabled at Ayr Townhead sidings. The Strathclyde orange livery was in use from 1986 until 2000. Taken September 1986.

No. 143015 (HT) at Dumfries station box after reversing to form a local service to Newcastle. Taken February 1986.

No. 143019 (HA) at Bathgate. This was only a single platform and was replaced by a new Bathgate station further east in 2010 when the through electric services between Bathgate and Airdrie were re-started. Taken April 1986.

No. 150001 (HQ) at Kilwinning with a Glasgow Central to Stranraer Harbour service. This was the first time a sprinter was tried out and was the forerunner of the later Class 156s that took over these services. Taken September 1985.

No. 303050 (HY) arrives at Glasgow Central with a service from Newton. Note the driver has already changed the destination board for its next working to Kirkhill. This unit was transferred to Crewe in 1981 and was not refurbished. It was withdrawn from traffic in 1990. Taken July 1976.

No. 303085 (GW) at Langside with a Glasgow Central to Kirkhill service. This unit was refurbished in 1984 and survived until 2000. Taken May 1980.

No. 303008 (GW) departs from Glasgow Central with a Cathcart Outer Circle service. This unit was the first 303 to receive the Strathclyde orange livery. Taken August 1987.

Six-car 311/303 combination, with unit No. 102 (HY) leading, at Newton with a Motherwell to Dalmuir via Singer service. Taken April 1986.

No. 104452 (AY) north of Kilwinning at Dalgarven with an Ayr to Glasgow Central service. Note the middle coach was a 107 trailer and the rear coach was a Class 120 power car. Taken April 1986.

No. 104456 (HA) in Edinburgh Waverley. This unit had just arrived on a service from Dunblane. Taken May 1987.

A Class 105/101 DMU combination arrives at Irvine with a Glasgow Central to Ayr service. Taken July 1986.

Three-car 107 at Paisley Canal with a Glasgow Central to Kilmacolm service. This service was withdrawn in January 1983. This was a very useful diversionary route when there were problems around the Paisley Gilmour Street area. Taken June 1980.

Six-car 107/116 combination, unit No. 148 (HM) leading, passes Dubbs Junction, south of Kilwinning, with a Glasgow Central to Largs service. Taken June 1981.

No. 107444 (AY) at Dunfermline Upper station. This was situated on the Dunfermline to Alloa line and was visited by a Branch Line Society Railtour that had been to several freight lines around the Fife area. Taken June 1984.

No. 116154 (HN) arrives at Glasgow Central with a service from Barrhead. These units were also known as high-density units with more doors per coach. Taken July 1976.

No. 116396 (HM) at its home depot of Hamilton. This depot was located close to Hamilton West station. It was closed in June 1982 and all DMUs were transferred to Ayr and Eastfield. Taken April 1982.

A Class 120/107/105/108/101/120 DMU combination at Brownhill, south of Glengarnock, with an Ayr to Glasgow Central service. Prior to the introduction of the Class 318s, Ayr depot used everything but the kitchen sink to keep services running! Taken May 1986.

Six-car 126, power car No. 51036 (AY) leading, departs from Troon station with a Glasgow Central to Ayr service. Taken May 1979.

Six-car 126 near Brownhill north of Dalry with an Ayr to Glasgow Central service. The third coach is No. SC51017, which was later saved along with three other 126 vehicles for preservation. Taken April 1980.

A general view of Ayr's Kyle Street, situated adjacent to the station. At this time Class 126s were the dominant traction, supported by Class 101 and 107 DMUs. These sidings were closed in early 1986 and are now a residential area. Taken September 1980.

Three-car 126 emerges from Mossgiel Tunnel south of Mauchline on the main G&SW line between Dumfries and Kilmarnock with the 14.10 Carlisle to Ayr service. Taken September 1980.

Six-car 126 approaches Irvine station on a bleak hogmanay with the 14.35 Glasgow Central to Ayr service. Taken December 1975.

Three-car 107 at Hunterston Low Level. This was another Branch Line Society Railtour, which visited many freight lines around Ayrshire. Taken August 1981.

Six-car 126, No. PC51039 leading, at Bogside, between Kilwinning and Irvine, with a Glasgow Central to Ayr service. Taken February 1981.

Three-car 126, No. PC51038 leading, passes its home depot of Ayr with a Glasgow Central to Ayr working. Taken March 1981.

No. 318256 (GW) at North Berwick, having just arrived with a service from Edinburgh. Class 318s were tried on this service but were deemed unsuitable and were later replaced by four-car Class 322s. Taken November 2001.

Eight-car 156, unit No. 437 (CK) leading, at Ayr with a Glasgow Central to Stranraer Harbour service. This service had been strengthened from four to eight cars due to rugby supporters going back to Ireland via Larne. Taken April 1989.

No. 156506 (CK) arrives at Maybole station with a Stranraer Harbour to Newcastle service. Taken April 1999.

No. 156477 (IS) at Platform 1 at Inverness with a Kyle of Lochalsh service. Taken March 2000.

Bridgeton Central Yard with 303 and 314 units. At this time electric units were stabled and washed only. This facility closed in 1987 when a new yard at Yoker took over. Taken May 1983.

Six-car 126, No. 413 unit leading, east of Paisley Gilmour Street with the 07.00 Ayr to Glasgow Central service. No. 126413 was the unit that was later preserved by the Swindon Diesel Preservation Society, based at Bo'ness, West Lothian. Taken May 1982.

No. 158802 (HT) arrives at Glasgow Central with a TransPennine service from Leeds. This service was withdrawn in 2006. Taken November 2002.

Four-car 220 near Auchinleck with a diverted Glasgow Central to Birmingham New Street service. This service had been diverted off the WCML due to engineering works. Taken March 2004.

No. 322481 (GW) approaches Prestonpans with an Edinburgh to North Berwick service. These units were replaced by Class 380s from May 2011. Taken March 2004.

No. 170421 (HA) at Linlithgow with an Edinburgh to Glasgow Queen Street service. Taken March 2004.

No. 158726 (HA) arrives at Polmont with an Edinburgh to Dunblane service. Taken March 2004.

A Class 390 *Pendilino* at Platform 1 Glasgow Central with a service to London Euston. Taken March 2004.

No. 170411 (HA) at Aberdeen, having just arrived with a service from Glasgow Queen Street. Taken June 2004.

No. 158720 (IS) arrives at Dyce with an Aberdeen to Inverurie service. Taken June 2004.

No. 158717 (IS) arrives at Inverness with a service from Aberdeen. Taken June 2004.

Five-car 220 at Haymarket with an Edinburgh to Paignton service. Taken April 2006.

No. 156430 (CK) at Girvan, having just arrived with a service from Ayr. Taken June 2006.

No. 70002 (FL) near Mauchline, on the G&SW, with MGR empties heading north to Killoch Colliery from Ratcliffe-on-Soar Power Station. Taken January 2011.

No. 170471 (HA) at Alloa, having just arrived with a service from Glasgow Queen Street. Taken June 2008.

No. 158868 (HA) arrives at Glasgow Queen Street with a service from Falkirk Grahamston. Taken May 2009.

No. 185147 (AK) departs Glasgow Central with a Manchester Airport service. Most of these services are now worked by electric Class 350s. Taken May 2009.

No. 314208 (GW) at Port Glasgow with a Gourock to Glasgow Central service. Taken November 2009.

No. 320301 (GW) at Helensburgh Central with a service to Airdrie. Taken April 2010.

No. 334032 (GW) arrives at Bathgate with an Edinburgh to Milngavie service. Taken May 2011.

No. 158869 (HA) departs Kirkwood station with a Whifflet to Glasgow Central service. This line was electrified in 2014. Taken May 2011.

No. 334035 (GW) arrives at Rutherglen station with a Motherwell to Balloch service. Note the new M74 motorway above the station. Taken August 2011.

No. 320309 (GW) at Hamilton Central station with a Larkhall to Dalmuir service. This unit was named *Radio Clyde 25th Anniversary*. Taken August 2011.

No. 380104 (GW) at Dunbar, ready to depart with a service to Edinburgh. Taken June 2012.

No. 334036 (GW) at Edinburgh with a service for Milngavie. Taken June 2012.

No. 58011 (TO) with No. 47972 (HQ) behind providing train heating at Dalgarven, near Kilwinning, with a Hertfordshire Railtour special from Preston to Waterside, south of Ayr. Taken September 1994.

Six-car 334, unit No. 004 (GW) leading, approaches Drumgelloch station with an Edinburgh to Helensburgh Central service. Taken June 2012.

No. 153317 (NH) outside Brodies Works, Kilmarnock, after a C3 refurbishment on behalf of Northern Rail. Taken January 2013.

Six-car 170, unit No. 404 (HA) leading, approaches Edinburgh Park station with an Edinburgh to Glasgow Queen Street service. Taken March 2004.

No. 221131 (CZ) at Glasgow Central, having arrived with a service from Derby. Taken February 2014.

No. 318251 (GW) at Cumbernauld with a service to Balloch. Taken May 2014.

No. 334011 (GW) at Easterhouse with a Milngavie to Edinburgh service. Taken May 2014.

No. 380110 (GW) arrives at Bridgeton station with a Rutherglen to Garscadden service. This was an additional service provided in connection with the Commonwealth Games. Taken July 2014.

No. 390052 (MA) is near Crawford with a Glasgow Central to London Euston service. Taken August 2014.

Eight-car 350, No. 409 leading (AK), is near Abington with a Glasgow Central to Manchester Airport service. Taken August 2014.

No. 67008 (TO) is stabled at the east end of Edinburgh Waverley between sleeper duties. Taken March 2004.

No. 170455 (HA) reaches the top of Cowlairs incline with a Glasgow Queen Street to Aberdeen service. Taken November 2014.

No. 380112 (GW) is at Dundonald, between Barassie and Irvine, with an Ayr to Glasgow Central service. Taken April 2015.

No. 170473 (HA) arrives at Edinburgh Park station with a Dunblane to Edinburgh service. Taken May 2015.

No. 156495 (CK) is near Hairmyres with an East Kilbride to Glasgow Central service. Taken July 2015.

Five-car 220 approaches Kirkconnel with a Carlisle to Glasgow Central special. This was a temporary service between January and February 2016 due to the West Coast Main Line being closed at Lamington due to storm damage to a bridge. Taken January 2016.

No. 56011 (TO) at Falkland Yard Ayr awaiting to depart with an empty MGR to Waterside. With the closure of most of the Ayrshire open-cast mines, Falkland Yard is now a ghost yard. Taken June 1998.

Nine-car 390 approaches Shieldmuir, south of Motherwell, with a Glasgow Central to London Euston service. Note the front protection cover is missing, which suggests that the unit had probably recently been assisted by a Thunderbird loco. Taken March 2016.

No. 170475 (HA) arrives at Glasgow Queen Street Low Level with a diverted service from Edinburgh. The High Level station was closed at this time due to major engineering work in connection with electrification. Taken June 2016.

No. 314212 (GW) at Williamwood station with a Neilston to Glasgow Central service. Taken October 2016.

No. 314207 (HY) at Balloch Central station with a High Street service. This station was closed in September 1986 as a result of the 1984 Strathclyde Rail Review. The *Maid of The Loch* boat had already ceased services on Loch Lomond in 1981. The new Balloch station was situated behind the camera, thus eliminating the level crossing. Taken August 1981.

Nos 303011/029/036, all allocated to Hyndland, await their next turn of duty at Milngavie station. The old Platform 3 on the left was closed in the early 1990s and part of the branch has been singled, making this a now badly congested line. Taken August 1981.

No. 140001 (HQ) at East Kilbride, having arrived on a service from Glasgow Central. This was the forerunner of the modern sprinters that were to follow. Taken August 1981.

Six-car 126, power car No. 51020 leading, at Shotts station. This unit was working a service to Hamilton West via Motherwell. Taken August 1981.

No. 303062 (HY) emerges out of Glasgow Queen Street tunnel towards the station with an Airdrie to Helensburgh Central service. Taken August 1981.

No. 105375 (HA) in Edinburgh on a Cowdenbeath service. Taken August 1981.

Three-car 126 passes Gatehead signal box near Kilmarnock with a Carlisle to Ayr service. This service ran from May 1979 until May 1983. Taken April 1982.

No. 126407 (AY) passes Hurlford signal box with the 09.10 Ayr to Carlisle service. Taken May 1982.

Three-car 105 at West Kilbride with the 14.52 Largs to Glasgow Central service. Taken November 1982.

Three-car 126, power car No. 51017 leading, at Kilwinning with the 15.52 Largs to Glasgow Central service. Taken November 1982.

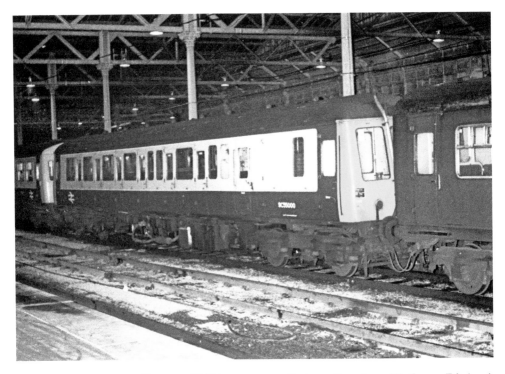

Gloucester DMU power car No. 55000 (HA) is seen as part of a six-car formation at Platform 13 Edinburgh with a set of ECS to Haymarket Depot. Taken February 1983.

No. 116387 (ED) at Falkirk Grahamston, having just arrived with a service from Glasgow Queen Street. Taken May 1983.

Dalry station before the bulldozers moved in. On the left a three-car 107 on the 14.00 Glasgow Central to Ayr is seen and on the right is another three-car 107, this time with a connecting service to Ardrossan Winton Pier. Taken October 1983.

Two-car 108 approaches Dumfries with a local service from Carlisle. Taken April 1982.

No. 303080 (GW) departs Paisley Gilmour Street with a Wemyss Bay to Glasgow Central service. Taken September 1986.

No. 170401 (HA) arrives at Montrose with an Aberdeen to Edinburgh service. Taken June 2001.

No. 104458 (HA) at Dunblane station, having just arrived with a service from Edinburgh. Taken August 1987.

Three-car 108 DMU, unit 383 (CK) leading, at Platform 3 Glasgow Central, having just arrived with a local service from Barrhead. This unit was on loan to Corkerhill Depot from Neville Hill, Leeds, to help out with shortages. Taken August 1988.

No. 120532, PC 53699 (AY), stabled at Corkerhill Depot awaits its next turn of duty. Taken April 1989.

Two-car 141 in Barclays Yard, Kilmarnock, awaiting movement into the sheds for repairs. Taken March 1989.

No. 142053 (NH) in the yard at Andrew Barclays, Kilmarnock, awaiting repairs. Taken March 1990.

Two-car 156 at Inverness with a service to Thurso and Wick. Taken June 1991.

No. 107444 (AY) at Markinch with a Branch Line Society Railtour from Edinburgh. Taken June 1984.

No. 156496 (CK) arrives at Crianlarich with a Glasgow Queen Street to Fort William service. Taken May 1992.

Four-car 156, including units 506 and 509 (both CK), on the Waterside Branch near Holybush with a branch line special from Ayr. These two units travelled extensively all over the south of Scotland that day including Ardrossan Harbour and Giffen. Taken July 1992.

No. 156439 (CK) passes the disused station of Thornhill with a Glasgow Central to Carlisle service. Taken February 1993.

Six-car 318, unit
260 (GW) leading,
approaches
Lochwinnoch station
with a Glasgow Central
to Ayr working. Taken
April 1993.

No. 936104 (GW) –
formerly No. 311104,
converted for Sandite
duties – arrives at
Kilwinning with a
southbound working to
Ayr. Taken March 1996.

Eight-car 325, unit 006
(WN) leading, arrives at
Glasgow Central with
a postal working from
London Wembley Yard.
Taken December 1996.

No. 185114 (AK)
arrives at Edinburgh
with a service from
Manchester Airport.
Taken February 2014.

No. 117308 (HA) arrives
at Edinburgh with a
service from Kirkcaldy.
Taken August 1998.

Six-car 158, unit 745
(HA) leading, at Perth
with an Inverness to
Edinburgh service.
Taken August 1998.

Four-car 158, unit
707 (HA) leading,
approaches Falkirk
Grahamston with a
Dunblane to Edinburgh
working. Taken
1 September 1999.

No. 303033 (GW)
stabled in the sidings
at Airdrie awaits its
next turn of duty. Taken
June 2001.

No. 170416 (HA)
approaches Dundee
with a Glasgow Queen
Street to Aberdeen
service. Taken July 2001.

No. 150258 (HA) arrives at Inverkeithing with an Edinburgh to Cowdenbeath working. Taken July 2001.

Four-car 158, unit 740 (HA) leading, at Stirling Middle signal box with an Aberdeen to Glasgow Queen Street service. Taken June 2001.

No. 92019 (CE) *Wagner* at Abington with the northbound Tesco express from Daventry to Grangemouth. Taken August 2014.

No. 37111 (ED) crosses Glenfinnan Viaduct with the 05.50 Glasgow Queen Street to Fort William service. This viaduct was made famous in later years with the Harry Potter movies. Taken February 1984.

No. 37415 (IS) at Inverness station with a service to Kyle of Lochalsh. This loco was renumbered from No. 37277 in November 1985. It lasted in service until May 2012 and was eventually cut up at C.F. Booth of Rotherham in November 2013.